# Your first 100 words in SPANISH

## Spanish for Total Beginners Through Puzzles and Games

*Series concept*
Jane Wightwick

*Illustrations*
Mahmoud Gaafar

*Spanish edition*
Lydia Goldsmith

### McGraw-Hill

Chicago   New York   San Francisco   Lisbon   London   Madrid   Mexico City
Milan   New Delhi   San Juan   Seoul   Singapore   Sydney   Toronto

D1533556

**Other titles in this series:**

Your First 100 Words in Arabic
Your First 100 Words in Chinese
Your First 100 Words in French
Your First 100 Words in German
Your First 100 Words in Greek
Your First 100 Words in Hebrew
Your First 100 Words in Italian
Your First 100 Words in Japanese
Your First 100 Words in Korean
Your First 100 Words in Russian

*McGraw-Hill*

*A Division of The McGraw·Hill Companies*

1 2 3 4 5 6 7 8 9 0   VLP/VLP   1 0 9 8 7 6 5 4 3 2

ISBN 0-07-139602-0

Printed and bound by Vicks Lithograph

Cover design by Nick Panos

McGraw-Hill books are available at special quantity discounts to use as premiums and sales promotions, or for use in corporate training programs. For more information, please write to the Director of Special Sales, Professional Publishing, McGraw-Hill, Two Penn Plaza, New York, NY 10121-2298. Or contact your local bookstore.

This book is printed on acid-free paper.

# ◎ CONTENTS

**Flashcards** (8 sheets of tear-out topic flashcards)

# ◎ HOW TO USE THIS BOOK

In this activity book you'll find 100 key Spanish words and phrases. All of the activities are designed specifically for developing confidence in the early stages of learning a language. Many of the activities are inspired by the kind of games used to teach children to read their own language: flashcards, matching games, memory games, joining exercises, anagrams, etc. This is not only a more effective method of learning new words, but also much more fun.

We've included an **Introduction** to get you started. This is a friendly introduction to Spanish pronunciation and spelling that will give you tips on how to say and memorize the words.

Then you can move on to the 8 **Topics**. Each topic presents essential words with pictures to help memorization. There is a pronunciation guide so you know how to say each word. These words are also featured in the tear-out **Flashcard** section at the back of the book. When you've mastered the words, you can go on to try the activities and games for that topic.

Finally, there's a **Round-up** section to review all your new words and the **Answers** to all the activities to check yourself.

Follow this 4-step plan for maximum success:

**1** Have a look at the key topic words with their pictures. Then tear out the flashcards and shuffle them. Put them Spanish side up. Try to say the word and remember what it means. Then turn the card over to check with the English.

**2** Put the cards English side up and try to say the Spanish word. Try the cards again each day both ways around. (When you can remember a card for 7 days in a row, you can file it!)

**3** Try out the activities and games for each topic. This will reinforce your recognition of the key words.

**4** After you have covered all the topics, you can try the activities in the Round-up section to test your knowledge of all the Spanish words in the book. You can also try shuffling all the 100 flashcards together to see how many you can remember.

This flexible and fun way of learning your first words in Spanish should give you a head start whether you're studying at home or in a group.

# ◎ INTRODUCTION

The purpose of this section is to introduce the basic principles of how Spanish is written and pronounced. If you understand these principles, you will have a head start when it comes to learning your first words. Concentrate on the main points. The details will come as you progress.

Have a quick look at this section and try to produce the sounds out loud, in a confident manner and then move on to the topics for some practice. As you work your way through the words in this activity book, you will find the spelling and pronunciation gradually start to come more naturally.

## ◎ Pronunciation tips

Many Spanish letters are pronounced in a similar way to their English equivalents, but here are some differences to watch out for. It is these differences that trip up the beginner so try to look over this list and say the words out loud using the pronunciation guide (underscoring indicates the stress: see page 6).

| | |
|---|---|
| **r** | a Spanish **r** is trilled like a Scottish *r* |
| **v** | half way between an English *v* and *b* |
| **z** | pronounced *s* as in "sat," e.g. **zapato** *sapato* (shoe) |
| **c** | **c** before **e** or **i** is pronounced *s* as in "sat," e.g. **cinturón** *seentooron* (belt); otherwise *k* as in "kettle," e.g. **caro** *karo* (expensive) |
| **j** | pronounced *h* as in "hat," e.g. **granja** *granha* (farm) |
| **g** | **g** before **e** or **i** is pronounced like **j**, i.e. *h* as in "hat," e.g. **ligero** *leehero* (light [weight]); otherwise *g* as in "get," e.g. **gato** *gato* (cat) |
| **h** | always silent, e.g. **hola** *ola* (hello) |
| **ll** | *lli* as in "mi*lli*on," e.g. **lluvia** *l-yooveeya* (rain) |
| **ñ** | *ni* as in "o*ni*on," e.g. **mañana** *manyana* (tomorrow) |
| **qu** | pronounced *k* as in "kettle," e.g. **aquí** *akee* (here) |
| **e** | pronounced like the English *e* as in "get" but also pronounced *eh* on the end of a word, e.g. **grande** *grandeh* (big). |
| **i** | like *ee* as in "f*ee*t," e.g. **silla** *seel-ya* (chair) |
| **u** | like *oo* as in "boot," e.g. **estufa** *estoofa* (stove); before another vowel, it it pronounced *oo*, e.g. **puerta** *pwerta* (door) |

✔ Many Spanish letters are pronounced the same as English, but some need special attention

✔ **h** is silent

✔ **e** at the end of a word is always pronounced, e.g. **grande** = *grandeh*

## Stress

Stress is the emphasis or the part of a word said slightly louder than the rest of the word (<u>fac</u>tory, <u>win</u>dow, <u>rab</u>bit). Stress is marked by underlining in the pronunciation:

**tapete** (rug), pronounced *ta<u>pe</u>teh*

**camisa** (shirt), pronounced *ka<u>mee</u>sa*

**cinturón** (belt), pronounced *seentoo<u>ron</u>*

## Accents

Spanish uses an accent ( ´ ) which is put over a vowel. Sometimes this accent is used to distinguish between two words with the same spelling and sometimes to show where the stress falls:

**sí** (yes), to distinguish it from **si** (if)

**cinturón** (belt), to show stress

## Punctuation

Spanish uses an upside-down question mark before a question as well as one after. The same is true of the exclamation mark:

**¿dónde?** (where?)

**¡padre!** (great!)

✔ Spanish has an accent: ´
✔ The accent can show word stress, e.g. **cinturón**
✔ Spanish uses an upside-down question mark and exclamation in front of the word/phrase

## Masculine and feminine

In English, the definite article is always "the," e.g. "the table," "the door," "the river." In Spanish, nouns (naming words like "table," "door," or "river") are either masculine or feminine and the definite article changes accordingly: **el**, for masculine (**el río**, "the river") or **la** for feminine (**la puerta**, "the door"). These change to **los** (masculine) or **las** (feminine) in the plural.

Words ending in **-o** are usually masculine and those ending in **-a** are usually feminine. Other words can be either. You will also find an example of a plural word in the 100 words: **los pantalones**, "the pants." It is important as you progress in Spanish to know whether a word is masculine or feminine and, for this reason, we have given the 100 words with their articles. Try to get used to learning new words in this way — it will help you later.

## Similar words

You probably already know more Spanish than you realize. There are many words that are similar to English. If you apply the principles of Spanish spelling and pronunciation in this introduction, you can say them like a local.

Here are some examples of words that are very similar in Spanish and English. With these words and the 100 key words in this book, you will already have made progress more quickly than you imagined possible.

**la televisión**, pronounced *televeesee<u>on</u>*

**la computadora**, pronounced *kompoota<u>do</u>ra*

**los shorts**, pronounced as the English

**el hotel**, pronounced *o<u>tel</u>*

**el autobús**, pronounced *aooto<u>boos</u>*

**el taxi**, pronounced as the English

**el teléfono**, pronounced *tele̲fono*

**el restaurante**, pronounced *resto̲rante*

**el elefante**, pronounced *ele̲fanteh*

**el león**, pronounced *le̲yon*

✔ Spanish nouns are either masculine (**el**) or feminine (**la**)

✔ Words ending in **-o** are usually masculine; those ending in **-a** are usually feminine

✔ There are many words similar in English and Spanish

## Spanish alphabet

Here is the complete Spanish alphabet with the names of the letters. These can be useful if you need to spell something – your own name for example.

| | | | | | |
|---|---|---|---|---|---|
| A | *ah* | J | *ho̲ta* | R | *ehrreh* |
| B | *beh* | K | *ka* | S | *eh̲seh* |
| C | *seh* | L | *eh̲leh* | T | *teh* |
| D | *deh* | M | *eh̲meh* | U | *oo* |
| E | *eh* | N | *eh̲nneh* | V | *veh* |
| F | *eh̲feh* | Ñ | *eh̲nyeh* | W | *do̲bleh veh* |
| G | *heh* | O | *oh* | X | *e̲kees* |
| H | *a̲cheh* | P | *peh* | Y | *ee gree̲yega* |
| I | *ee* | Q | *koo* | Z | *se̲ta* |

# ① AROUND THE HOME

Look at the pictures of things you might find in a house.
Tear out the flashcards for this topic.
Follow steps 1 and 2 of the plan in the introduction.

**la ventana**
*la ventana*

**la silla**
*la seel-ya*

**la mesa**
*la mesa*

**el tapete**
*el tapeteh*

**el sofá**   *el sofa*

**la computadora**
*la kompootadora*

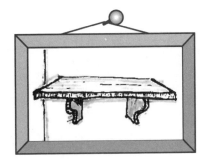

**el estante**
*el estanteh*

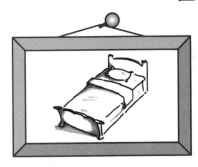

**la cama**   *la kama*

**el refrigerador**
*el refreeherador*

**la alacena**
*la alasena*

**la estufa**
*la estoofa*

**la puerta**
*la pwerta*

**9**

## ◎ **M**atch the pictures with the words, as in the example.

el sofá

la cama

la ventana

la mesa

el tapete

la computadora

el estante

la silla

---

## ◎ **N**ow match the Spanish household words to the English.

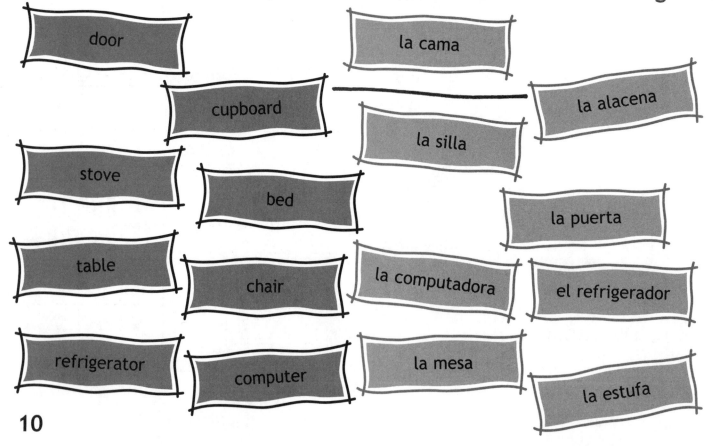

door

la cama

cupboard

la alacena

la silla

stove

bed

la puerta

table

chair

la computadora

el refrigerador

refrigerator

computer

la mesa

la estufa

◎ **F**ill in the missing letters in these household words.

s _ l _ _          s _ f _

r _ f _ i _ _ ra _ _ _          _ l _ c _ n _

v _ n t _ n _          m _ s _

e _ t _ f _          t _ _ e t _

_ u _ r _ _          e _ _ a n _ _

- - - - - - - - - - - - - - - - - - - - - - - -

◎ **S**ee if you can find these objects in the word square.
The words can run left to right, or top to bottom:

| B | A | T | A | P | I | S | D |
|---|---|---|---|---|---|---|---|
| I | P | U | E | R | T | A | A |
| C | R | L | S | R | V | T | A |
| V | E | N | T | A | N | A | L |
| C | R | A | U | E | L | P | L |
| A | T | C | F | A | I | E | E |
| M | E | S | A | D | T | T | E |
| A | S | I | L | L | A | E | B |

Decide where the household items should go. Then write the correct number in the picture, as in the example.

1 la mesa        2 la silla        3 el sofá        4 el tapete

5 el estante     6 la cama         7 la alacena     8 la estufa

9 el refrigerador  10 la computadora  11 la ventana   12 la puerta

Choose the Spanish word that matches the picture and fill in the English word at the bottom of the page.

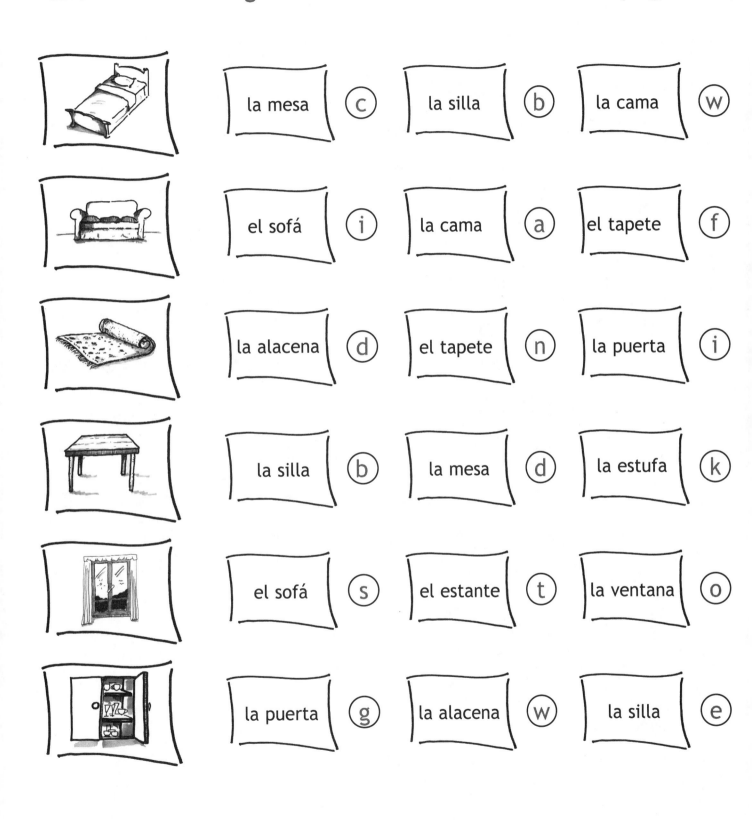

la mesa (c)   la silla (b)   la cama (w)

el sofá (i)   la cama (a)   el tapete (f)

la alacena (d)   el tapete (n)   la puerta (i)

la silla (b)   la mesa (d)   la estufa (k)

el sofá (s)   el estante (t)   la ventana (o)

la puerta (g)   la alacena (w)   la silla (e)

English word:   (w) ( ) ( ) ( ) ( ) ( )

13

# ② CLOTHES

Look at the pictures of different clothes.
Tear out the flashcards for this topic.
Follow steps 1 and 2 of the plan in the introduction.

**el cinturón**
*el seentooron*

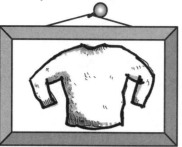

**el suéter**
*el sweter*

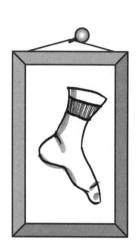

**el calcetín**
*el kalseteen*

**la bufanda**
*la boofanda*

**los pantalones**
*los pantalones*

**la corbata**
*la korbata*

**el vestido**
*el vesteedo*

**el zapato**
*el sapato*

**el abrigo**
*el abreego*

**la falda**
*la falda*

**el sombrero**
*el sombrero*

**la camisa** *la kameesa*

# Unscramble the letters to spell items of clothing.

Write the words with *el*, *la*, or *los*.

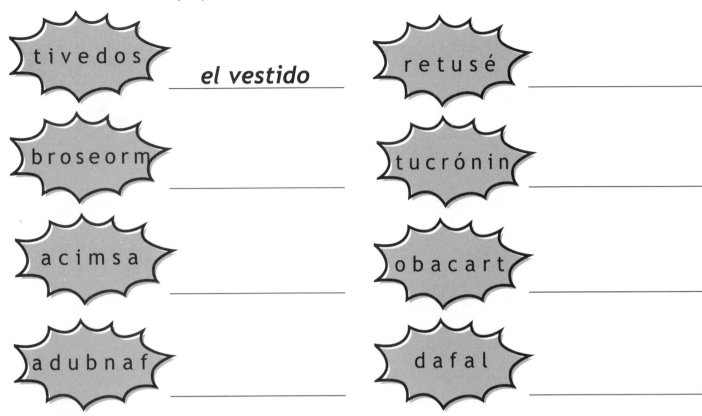

| | |
|---|---|
| t i v e d o s | el vestido |
| b r o s e o r m | |
| a c i m s a | |
| a d u b n a f | |
| r e t u s é | |
| t u c r ó n i n | |
| o b a c a r t | |
| d a f a l | |

- - - - - - - - - - - - - - - - - - - - - - - - - - - - - - - - - -

# See if you can find these clothes in the word square.

The words can run left to right, or top to bottom:

| F | A | P | F | A | L | D | A |
|---|---|---|---|---|---|---|---|
| C | O | R | B | A | T | A | B |
| A | H | S | U | É | T | E | R |
| M | E | L | M | E | B | S | I |
| I | M | A | N | T | E | A | G |
| S | V | E | S | T | I | D | O |
| A | S | O | U | S | U | O | E |
| H | E | R | A | E | N | N | T |

Now match the Spanish words, their pronunciation, and the English meaning, as in the example.

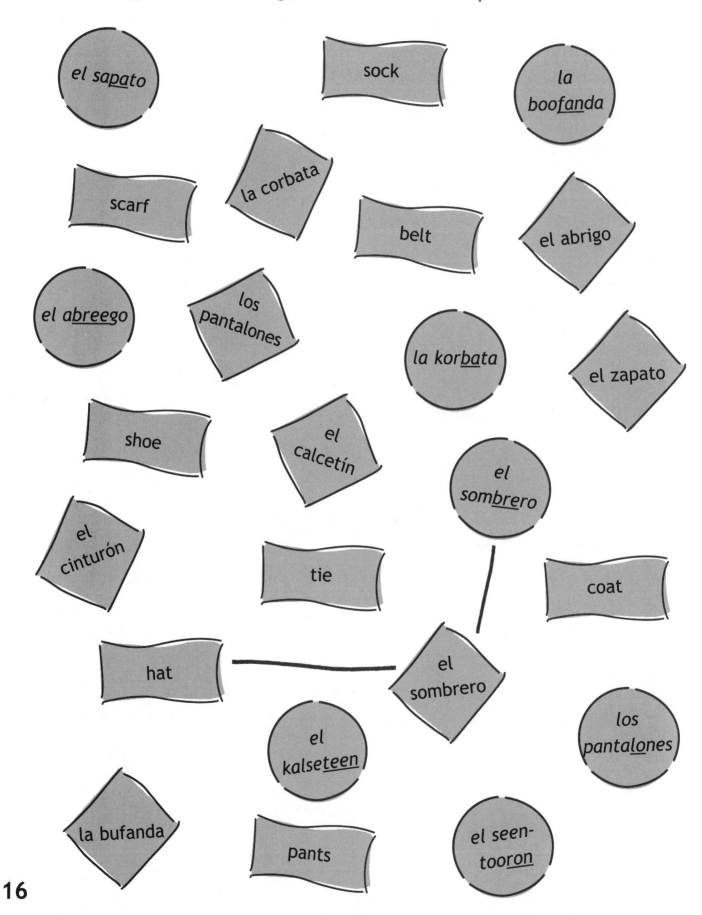

el sapato

sock

la boofanda

scarf

la corbata

belt

el abrigo

el abreego

los pantalones

la korbata

el zapato

shoe

el calcetín

el sombrero

el cinturón

tie

coat

hat

el sombrero

el kalseteen

los pantalones

la bufanda

pants

el seen-tooron

Carl is going on vacation. Count how many of each type of clothing he is packing in his suitcase.

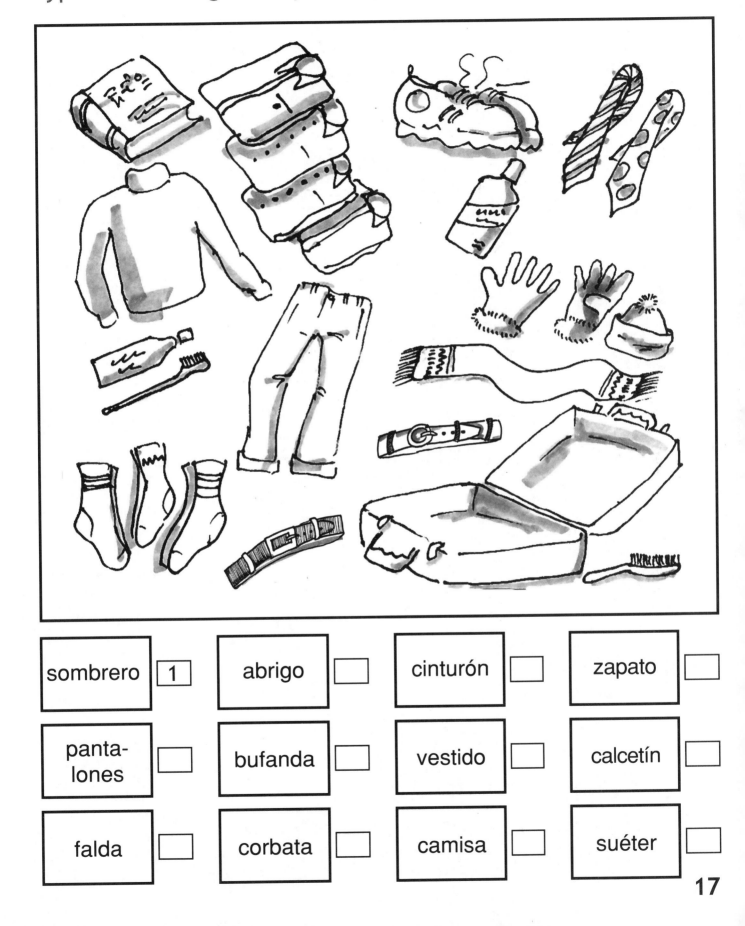

| | | | | | | |
|---|---|---|---|---|---|---|
| sombrero | 1 | abrigo | | cinturón | | zapato | |
| panta-lones | | bufanda | | vestido | | calcetín | |
| falda | | corbata | | camisa | | suéter | |

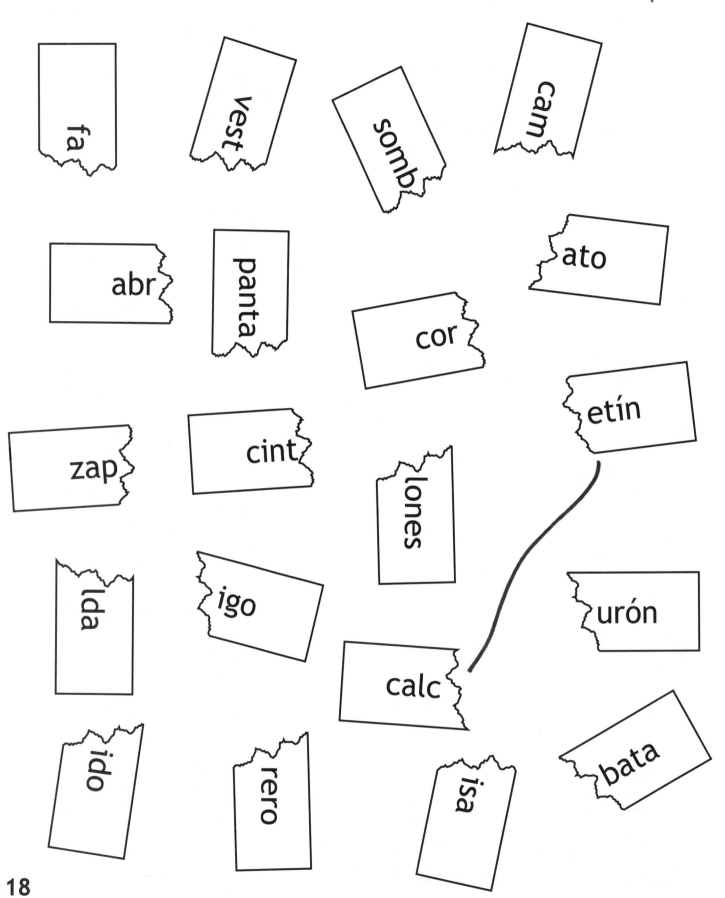

Someone has ripped up the Spanish words for clothes. Can you join the two halves of the words, as the example?

fa

Vest

somb

cam

abr

panta

ato

cor

etín

zap

cint

lones

lda

igo

urón

calc

ido

rero

isa

bata

# ❸ AROUND TOWN

Look at the pictures of things you might find around town.
Tear out the flashcards for this topic.
Follow steps 1 and 2 of the plan in the introduction.

## la fábrica
*la fabreeka*

## la panadería
*la panadereeya*

## la casa
*la kasa*

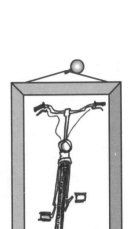

## la bicicleta
*la beeseekleta*

## el coche
*el kocheh*

## el camión
*el kameeyon*

## la fuente
*la fwenteh*

## la escuela  *la eskwela*

## la calle  *la kal-yeh*

## el banco  *el banko*

## la tienda  *la teeyenda*

## la carnicería
*la karneesereeya*

◎ **M**atch the Spanish words to their English equivalents.

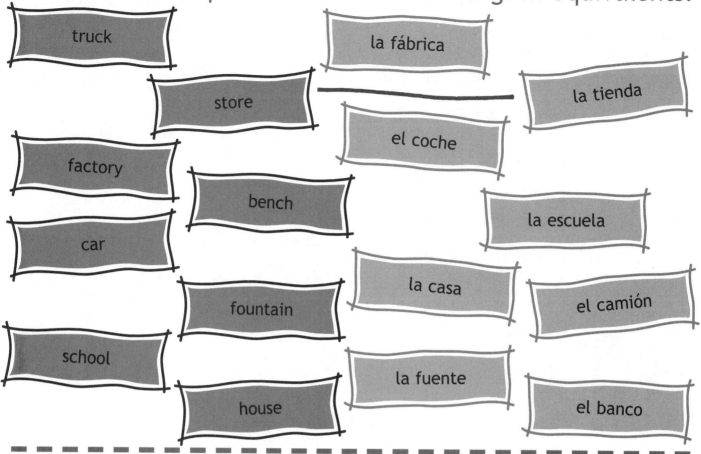

truck

la fábrica

store ———————— la tienda

el coche

factory

bench

la escuela

car

la casa

el camión

fountain

school

la fuente

el banco

house

- - - - - - - - - - - - - - - - - - - - - - - - - - - - - - - - - - - - - -

◎ **N**ow put the English words in the same order as the Spanish word chain, as in the example.

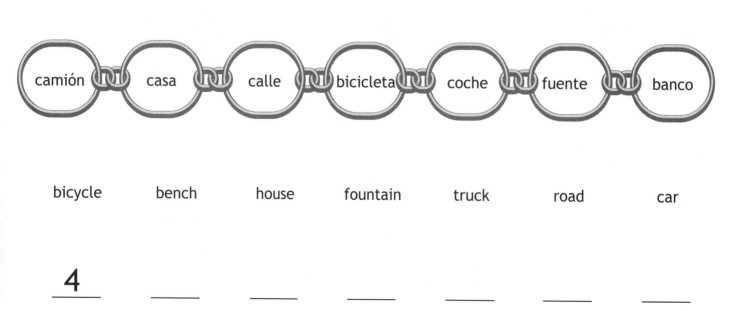

camión — casa — calle — bicicleta — coche — fuente — banco

bicycle      bench      house      fountain      truck      road      car

4  __  __  __  __  __  __

20

@ **L**abel this town plan, as in the example.

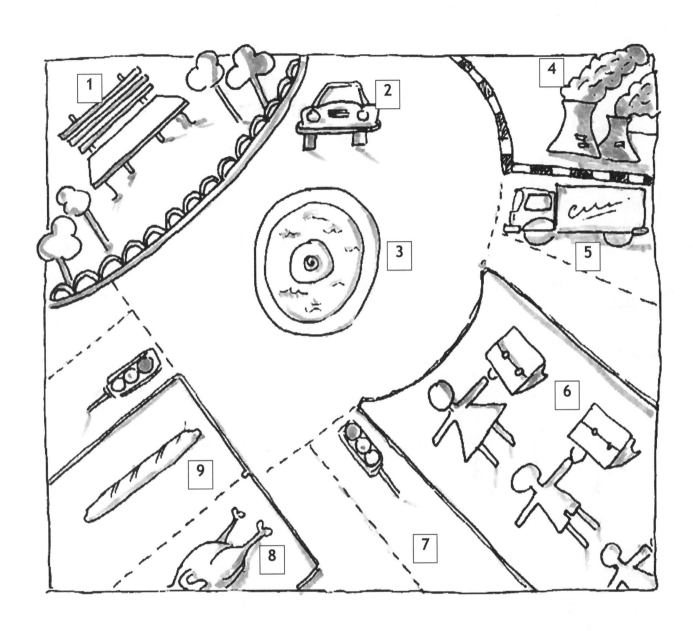

1 *el banco* _____ 2 _____ 3 _____

4 _____ 5 _____ 6 _____

7 _____ 8 _____ 9 _____

Choose the Spanish word that matches the picture and fill in the English word at the bottom of the page.

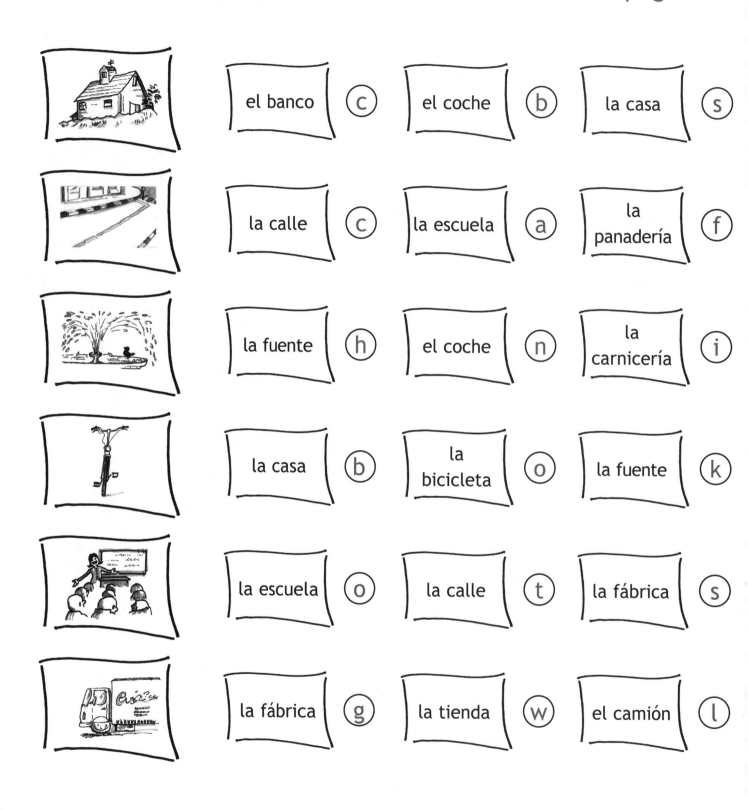

| | | |
|---|---|---|
| el banco (c) | el coche (b) | la casa (s) |
| la calle (c) | la escuela (a) | la panadería (f) |
| la fuente (h) | el coche (n) | la carnicería (i) |
| la casa (b) | la bicicleta (o) | la fuente (k) |
| la escuela (o) | la calle (t) | la fábrica (s) |
| la fábrica (g) | la tienda (w) | el camión (l) |

English word: (s) ( ) ( ) ( ) ( ) ( )

22

◎ **W**rite the words in the correct column, as in the example.

| el | la |
|---|---|
| *el banco* | |

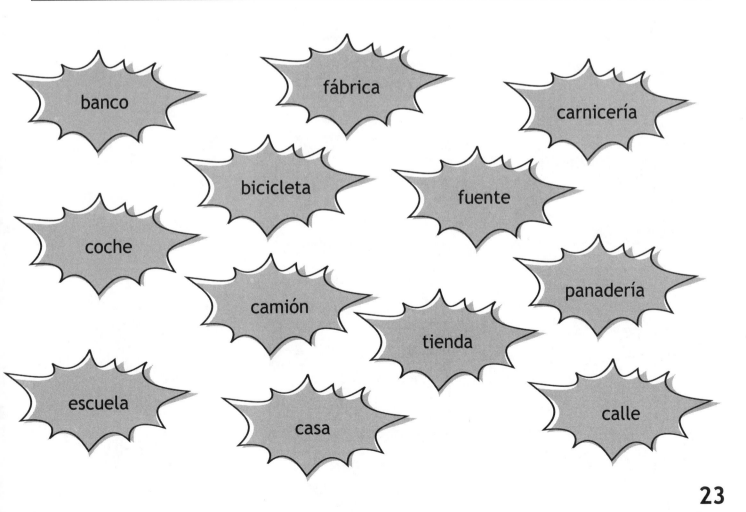

banco

fábrica

carnicería

bicicleta

fuente

coche

panadería

camión

tienda

escuela

casa

calle

# ④ COUNTRYSIDE

Look at the pictures of features you might find in the countryside.
Tear out the flashcards for this topic.
Follow steps 1 and 2 of the plan in the introduction.

## la colina
*la koleena*

## el puente
*el pwenteh*

## la granja
*la granha*

## la montaña
*la montanya*

## el lago
*el lago*

## el árbol
*el arbol*

## la flor
*la flor*

## el río   *el reeyo*

## el mar   *el mar*

## el campo   *el kampo*

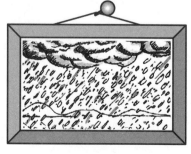

## la lluvia
*la l-yooveeya*

## el bosque
*el boskeh*

24

# Can you match all the countryside words to the pictures.

la montaña

la granja

el mar

el bosque

la lluvia

la colina

el lago

el puente

el río

la flor

el árbol

el campo

◎ **N**ow check (✔) the features you can find in this landscape.

| | | | | | | | |
|---|---|---|---|---|---|---|---|
| puente | ✔ | árbol | ☐ | lluvia | ☐ | colina | ☐ |
| montaña | ☐ | mar | ☐ | campo | ☐ | bosque | ☐ |
| lago | ☐ | río | ☐ | flor | ☐ | granja | ☐ |

◎ **U**nscramble the letters to reveal natural features.

Write the words with *el* or *la*.

luiluv — *la lluvia*

quesob — _____

boárl — _____

arm — _____

lorf — _____

íro — _____

galo — _____

alocin — _____

- - - - - - - - - - - - - - - - - - - -

◎ **S**ee if you can find 8 countryside words in the square.

The words can run left to right, or top to bottom:

| M | L | L | C | M | A | P | C |
|---|---|---|---|---|---|---|---|
| I | L | A | C | A | M | P | O |
| F | U | G | G | R | B | N | L |
| F | L | O | R | E | R | T | I |
| L | L | U | V | I | A | R | N |
| A | M | O | N | T | A | Ñ | A |
| C | O | N | J | A | Ñ | A | E |
| P | E | P | U | E | N | T | E |

© **F**inally, test yourself by joining the Spanish words, their pronunciation, and the English meanings, as in the example.

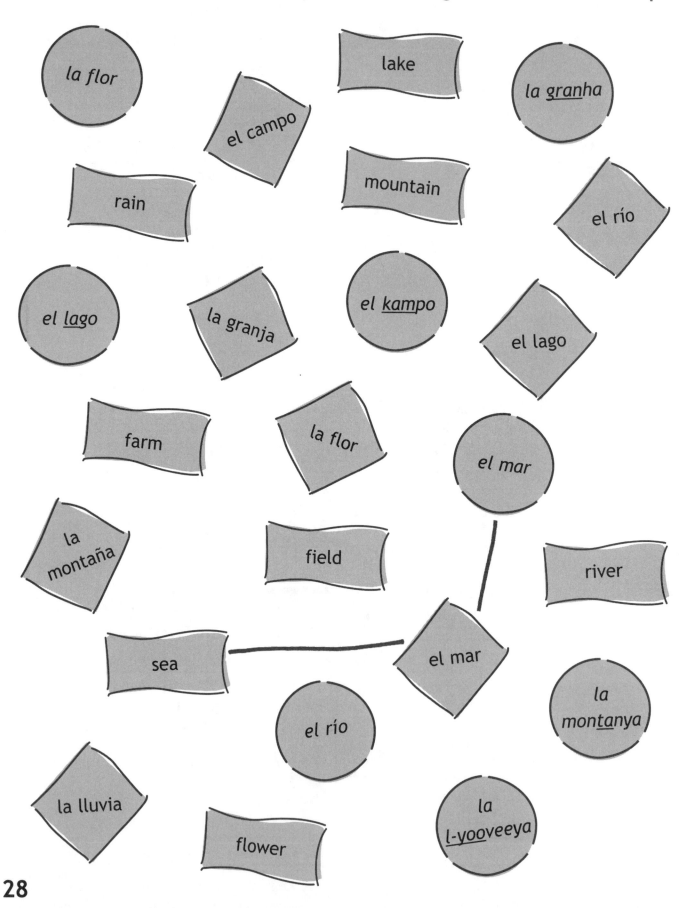

# ⑤ OPPOSITES

Look at the pictures.
Tear out the flashcards for this topic.
Follow steps 1 and 2 of the plan in the introduction.

sucio
*sooseeyo*

limpio
*leempeeyo*

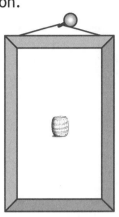

pequeño
*pekenyo*

grande
*grandeh*

barato
*barato*

ligero *leehero*

lento *lento*

caro *karo*

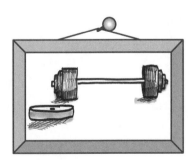

pesado *pesado*

rápido *rapeedo*

viejo *veeyeho*

nuevo *nwevo*

29

# Join the Spanish words to their English equivalents.

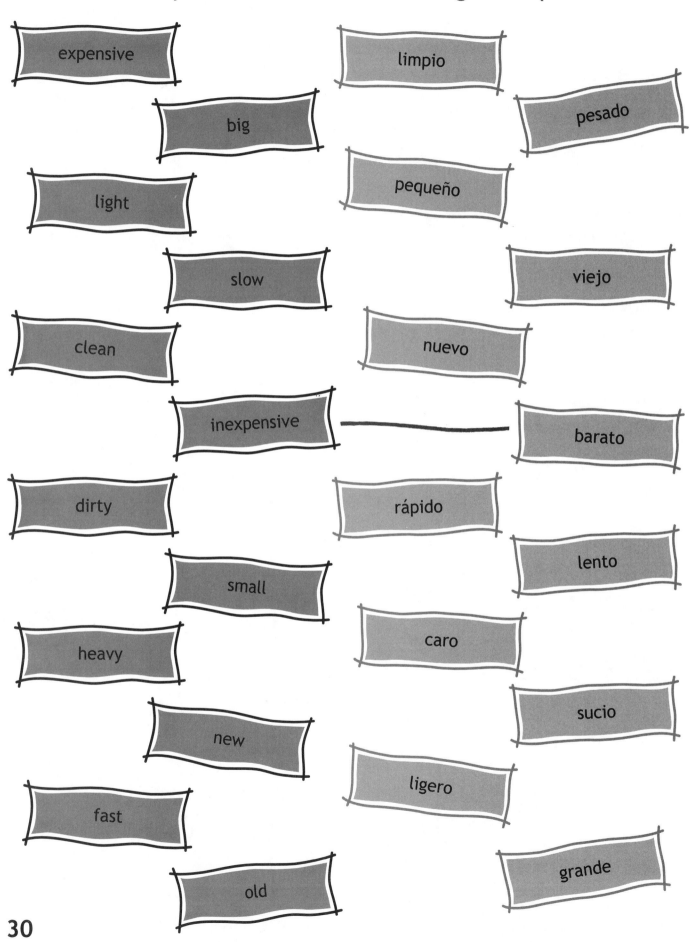

expensive

limpio

big

pesado

pequeño

light

slow

viejo

clean

nuevo

inexpensive ———— barato

dirty

rápido

lento

small

heavy

caro

sucio

new

ligero

fast

old

grande

Now choose the Spanish word that matches the picture to fill in the English word at the bottom of the page.

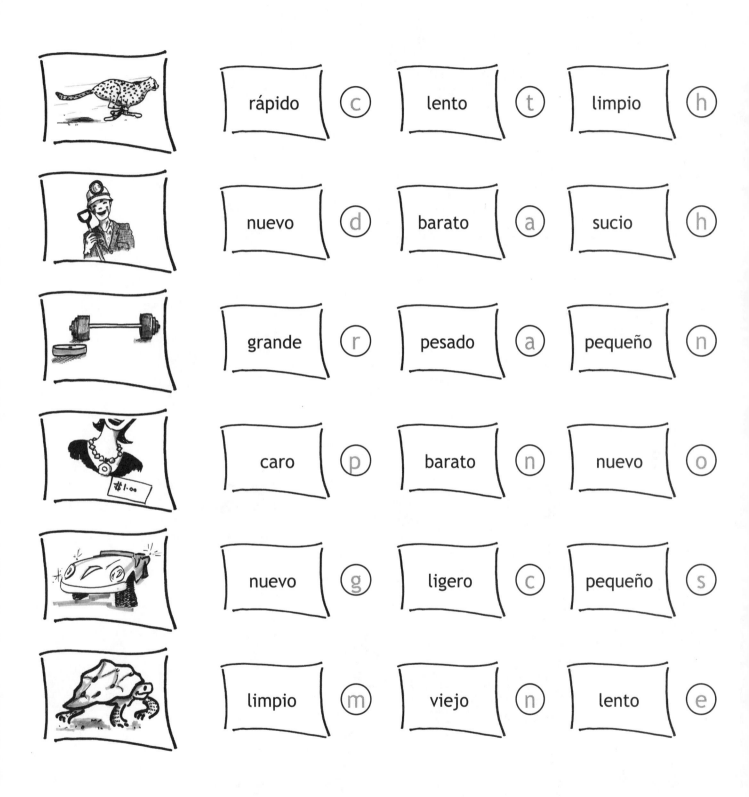

English word: ⓒ ◯ ◯ ◯ ◯ ◯

# Find the odd one out in these groups of words.

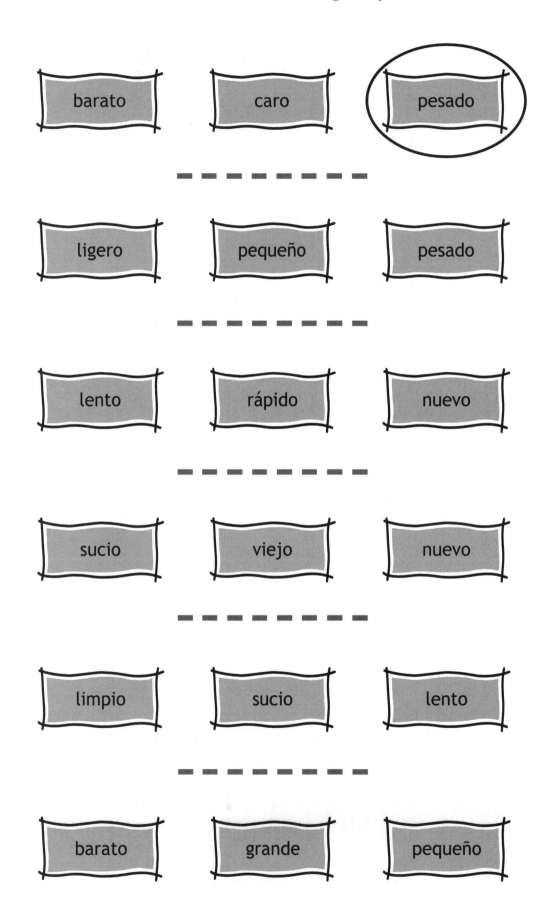

| barato | caro | (pesado) |
|--------|------|----------|

| ligero | pequeño | pesado |
|--------|---------|--------|

| lento | rápido | nuevo |
|-------|--------|-------|

| sucio | viejo | nuevo |
|-------|-------|-------|

| limpio | sucio | lento |
|--------|-------|-------|

| barato | grande | pequeño |
|--------|--------|---------|

Finally, join the English words to their Spanish opposites, as in the example.

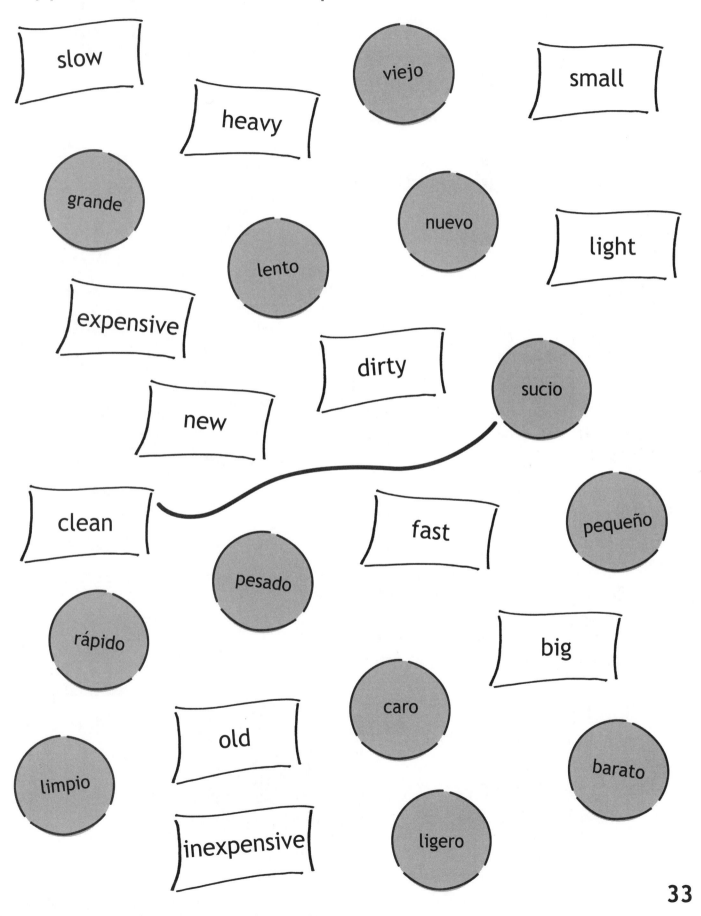

slow

viejo

small

heavy

grande

nuevo

light

lento

expensive

dirty

sucio

new

clean

fast

pequeño

pesado

rápido

big

caro

old

barato

limpio

inexpensive

ligero

# ⑥ ANIMALS

Look at the pictures.
Tear out the flashcards for this topic.
Follow steps 1 and 2 of the plan in the introduction.

el pato   *el pato*

## el burro
*el boorro*

## el gato
*el gato*

## el perro
*el perro*

## el conejo
*el koneho*

## el chango
*el chan-go*

## el pescado   *el peskado*

## el borrego   *el borrego*

## el ratón   *el raton*

## la vaca   *la vaka*

## el caballo
*el kabal-yo*

## el toro
*el toro*

34

◎ **M**atch the animals to their associated pictures, as in the example.

el conejo

el chango

el caballo

el gato

el borrego

el ratón

el perro

la vaca

el pescado

Someone has ripped up the Spanish words for animals.
Can you join the two halves of the words, as the example?

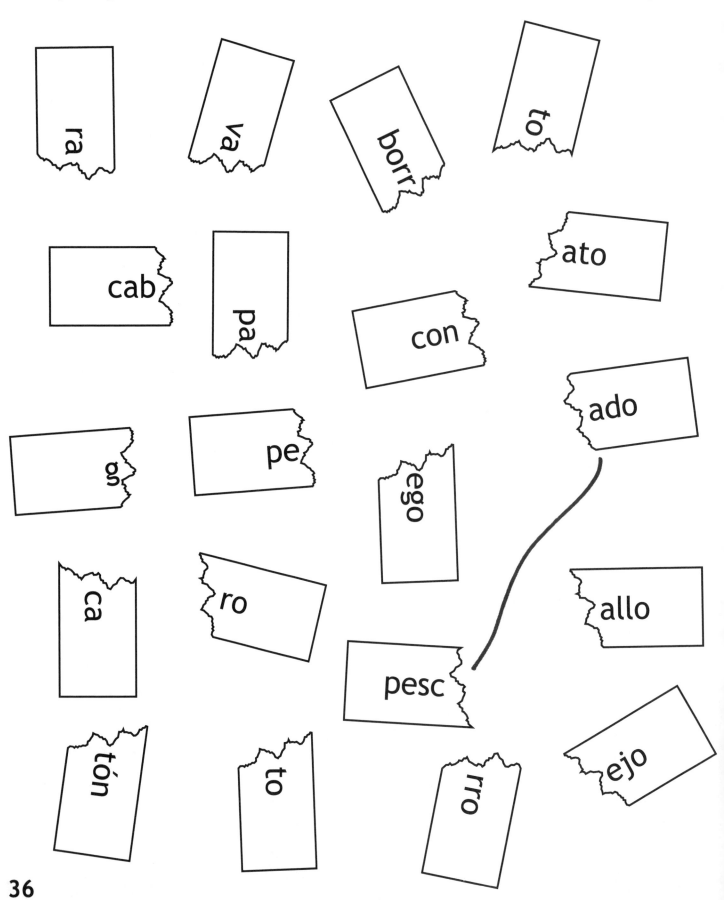

ra

va

borr

to

cab

pa

ato

con

g

pe

ego

ado

ca

ro

allo

pesc

tón

to

rro

ejo

⊚ **C**heck (✔) the animal words you can find in the word pile.

el lago

el gato

lento

el coche

el conejo

el burro

el borrego

la cama

pesado

la calle

la tienda

la falda

la colina

el toro

la vaca

el pescado

✔

## Join the Spanish animals to their English equivalents.

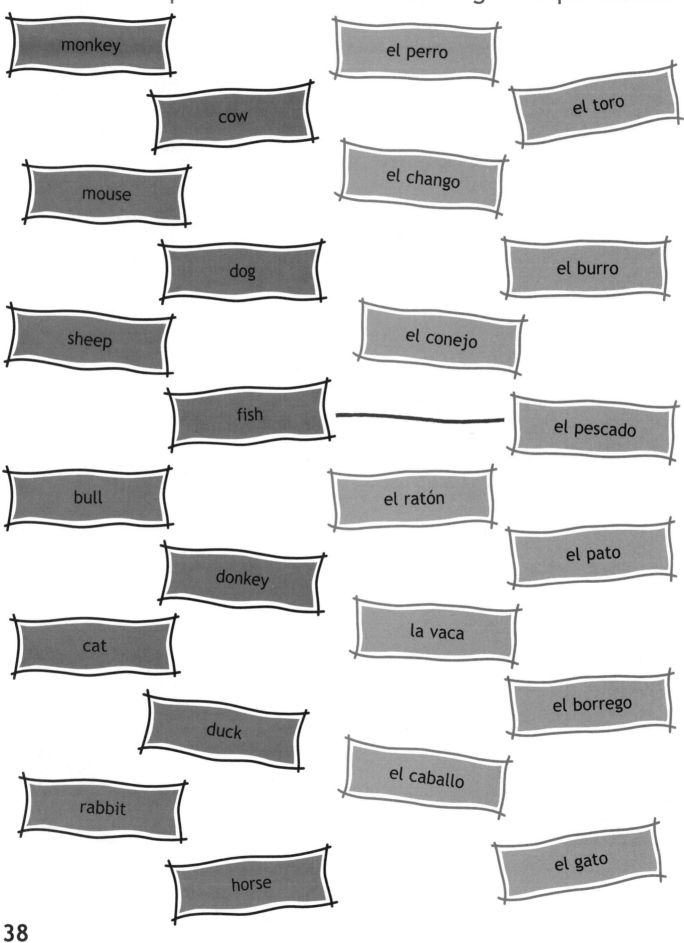

monkey

el perro

el toro

cow

el chango

mouse

dog

el burro

sheep

el conejo

fish —————— el pescado

bull

el ratón

donkey

el pato

cat

la vaca

duck

el borrego

rabbit

el caballo

horse

el gato

38

# 7 PARTS OF THE BODY

Look at the pictures of parts of the body.
Tear out the flashcards for this topic.
Follow steps 1 and 2 of the plan in the introduction.

el dedo
*el dedo*

la cabeza
*la kabesa*

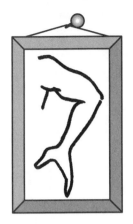

el brazo
*el braso*

el ojo   *el oho*

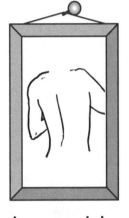

la espalda
*la espalda*

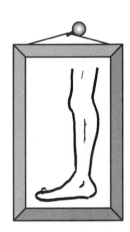

la pierna
*la pee-yerna*

la mano
*la mano*

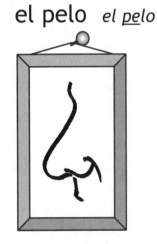

el pelo   *el pelo*

el estómago
*el estomago*

la oreja
*la oreha*

la boca
*la boka*

la nariz
*la naris*

39

◎ **M**atch the pictures with the words, as in the example.

la cabeza

el estómago

el brazo

el ojo

la mano

el pelo

el dedo

la espalda

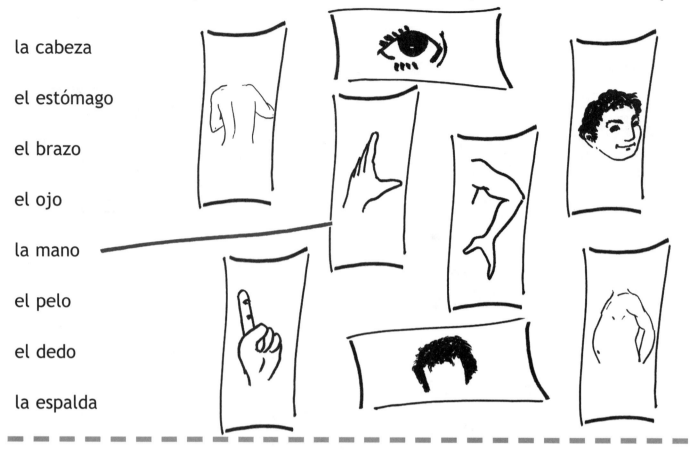

- - - - - - - - - - - - - - - - - - - - - - - - - - - - - - - - - - - - -

◎ **S**ee if you can find and circle six parts of the body in the word square, then draw them in the boxes below.

The words can run left to right, or top to bottom:

| S | N | H | E | V | B | U | G |
|---|---|---|---|---|---|---|---|
| I | A | M | A | N | O | B | I |
| C | R | L | D | S | C | O | V |
| P | I | E | R | N | A | U | A |
| E | Z | A | U | I | L | C | N |
| L | N | N | A | R | I | S | E |
| O | R | E | J | A | L | E | E |
| L | E | Z | P | R | T | A | T |

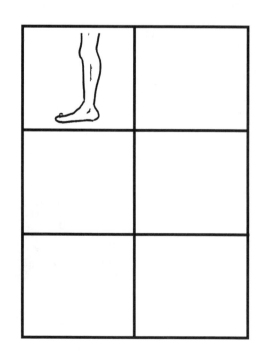

**40**

◎ **W**rite the words in the correct column, as in the example.

| el | la |
|---|---|
| *la nariz* | |

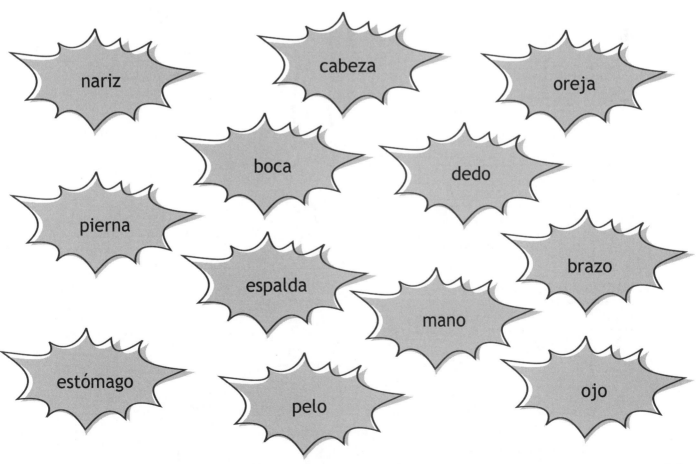

nariz

cabeza

oreja

boca

dedo

pierna

espalda

brazo

mano

estómago

pelo

ojo

◎ **L**abel the body with the correct number, and write *el* or *la* in front of the words.

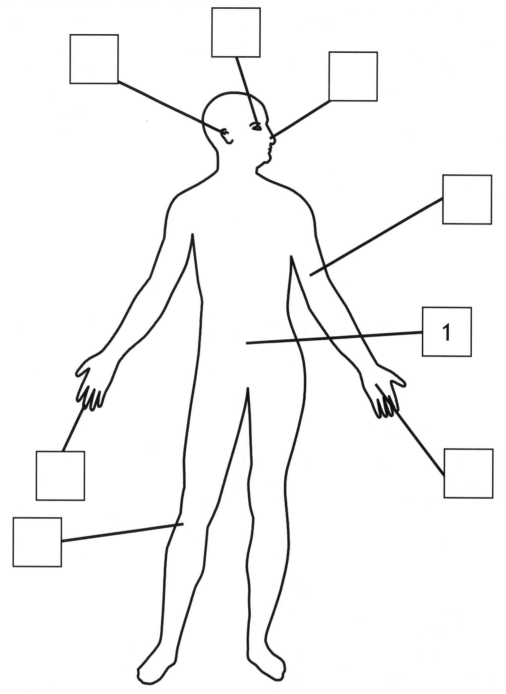

1 ___ estómago

2 ___ brazo

3 ___ nariz

4 ___ mano

5 ___ oreja

6 ___ pierna

7 ___ ojo

8 ___ dedo

Finally, match the Spanish words, their pronunciation, and the English meanings, as in the example.

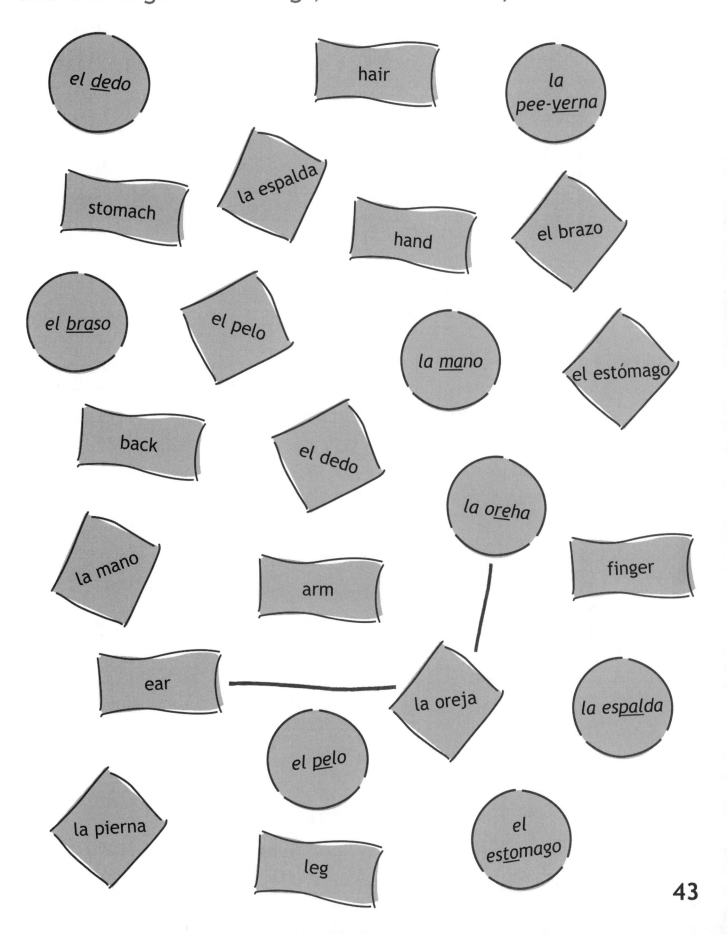

el dedo

hair

la pee-yerna

stomach

la espalda

hand

el brazo

el braso

el pelo

la mano

el estómago

back

el dedo

la oreha

la mano

arm

finger

ear

la oreja

la espalda

el pelo

la pierna

leg

el estomago

# 8 USEFUL EXPRESSIONS

Look at the pictures.
Tear out the flashcards for this topic.
Follow steps 1 and 2 of the plan in the introduction.

¿dónde? *dondeh*

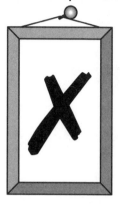

no
*no*

sí
*see*

hola *ola*

adiós
*adeeyos*

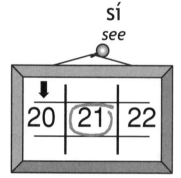

ayer
*ayer*

hoy
*oy*

mañana
*manyana*

aquí
*akee*

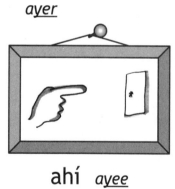

ahí *ayee*

ahora
*aora*

¿cuánto?
*kwanto*

perdón *perdon*

¡padre!
*padreh*

por favor
*por favor*

gracias
*graseeyas*

## ◎ Match the Spanish words to their English equivalents.

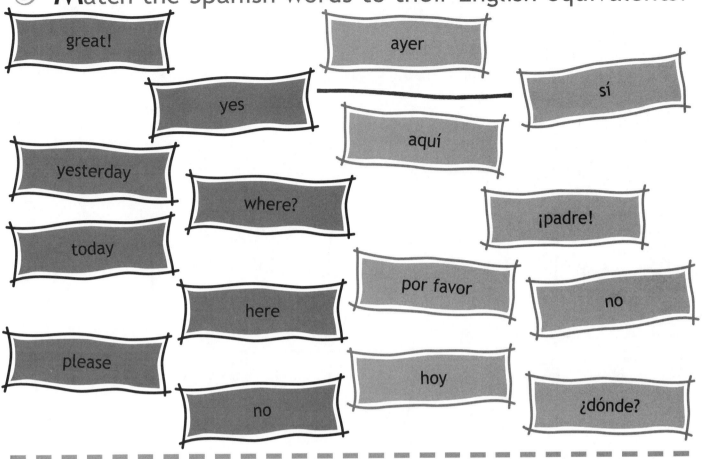

great!    ayer    sí

yes    aquí

yesterday    where?    ¡padre!

today    por favor    no

here

please    hoy    ¿dónde?

no

## ◎ Fill in the missing letters in these expressions.

¿c _ á _ t _?           _ _ y

_ r a _ i _ s           _ d _ ó _

p _ r _ ó _           ¡ _ a _ r _ !

_ o _ a           _ _ í

m _ ñ _ n _           a _ _ r _

45

Choose the Spanish word that matches the picture to fill in the English word at the bottom of the page.

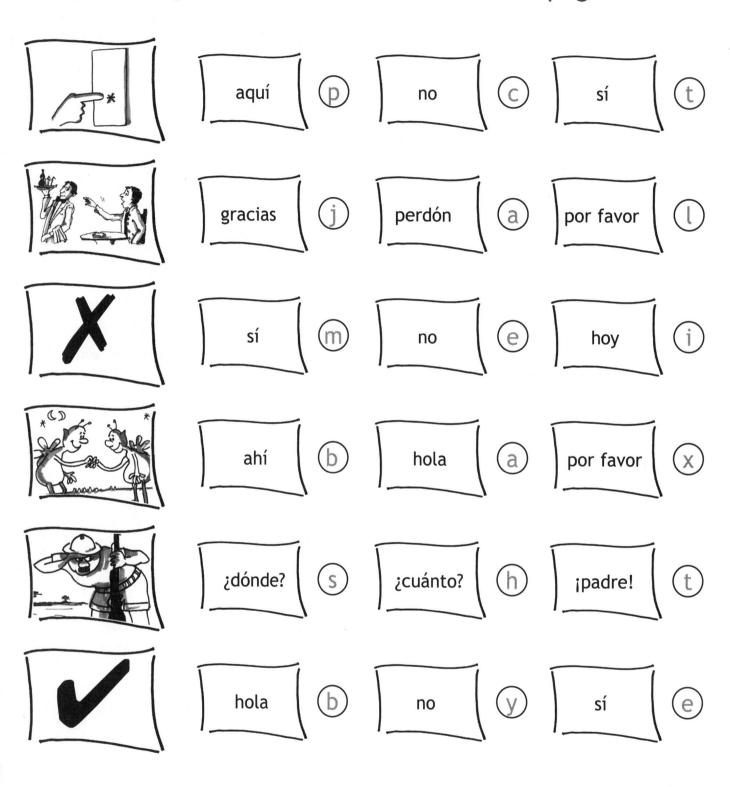

| | | |
|---|---|---|
| aquí (p) | no (c) | sí (t) |
| gracias (j) | perdón (a) | por favor (l) |
| sí (m) | no (e) | hoy (i) |
| ahí (b) | hola (a) | por favor (x) |
| ¿dónde? (s) | ¿cuánto? (h) | ¡padre! (t) |
| hola (b) | no (y) | sí (e) |

English word: (p) ( ) ( ) ( ) ( ) ( )

What are these people saying? Write the correct
number in each speech bubble, as in the example.

1 hola       2 por favor     3 sí        4 no

5 aquí       6 perdón        7 ¿dónde?   8 ¿cuánto?

Finally, match the Spanish words, their pronunciation, and the English meanings, as in the example.

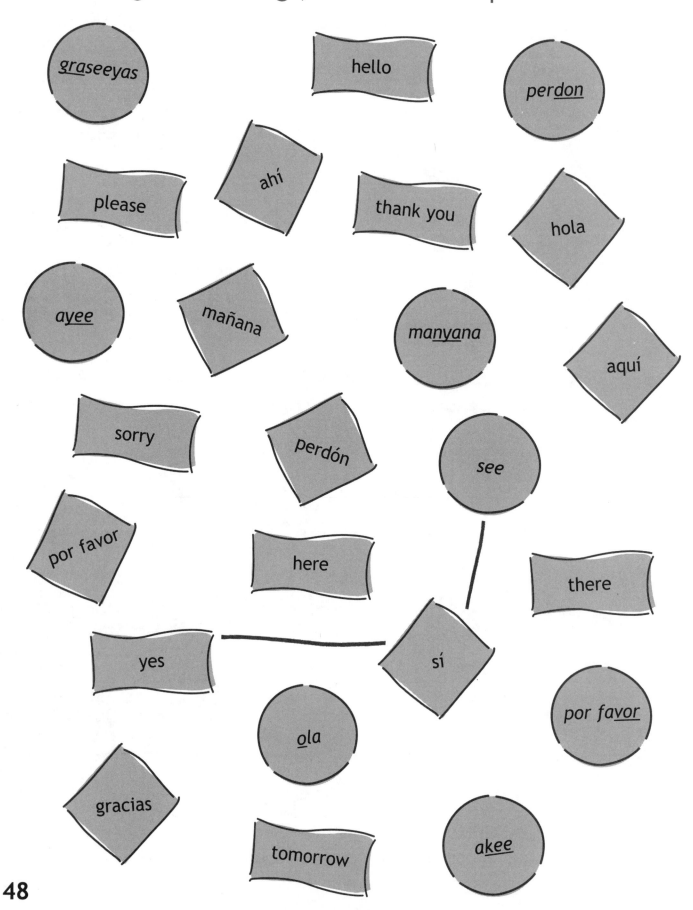

# ● ROUND-UP

This section is designed to review all the 100 words you have met in the different topics. It is a good idea to test yourself with your flashcards before trying this section.

◎ The ten objects below are all in the picture. Can you find and circle them?

| la puerta | la flor | la cama | el abrigo | el sombrero |

| la bicicleta | la silla | el perro | el pescado | el calcetín |

See if you can remember all these words.

hoy

la panadería

rápido

la nariz

la lluvia

sí

la alacena

el toro

el vestido

barato

el río

la pierna

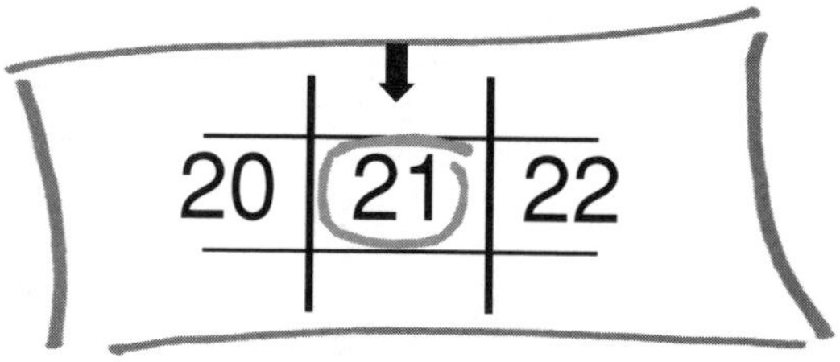

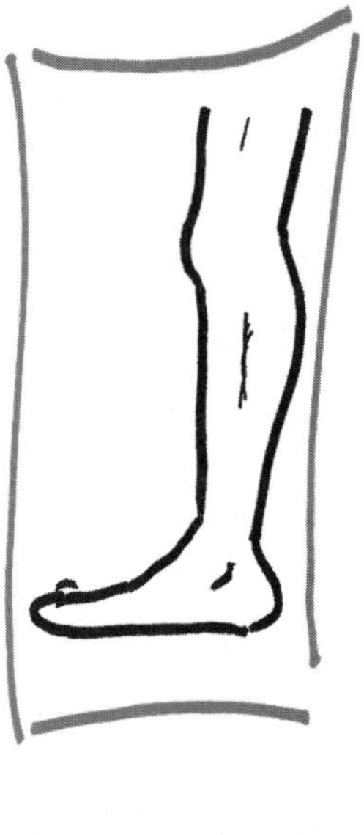

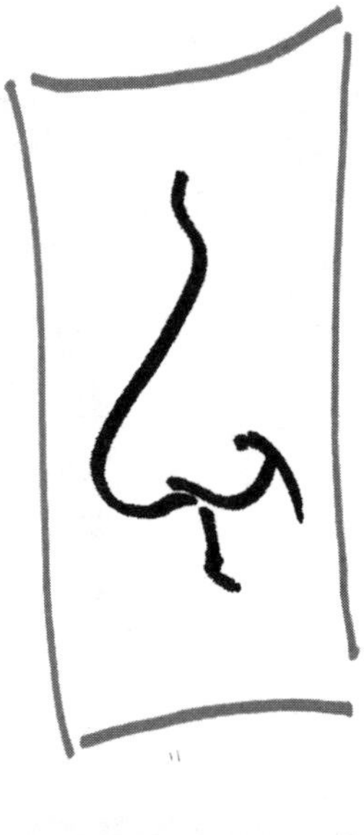

◎ **F**ind the odd one out in these groups of words and say why.

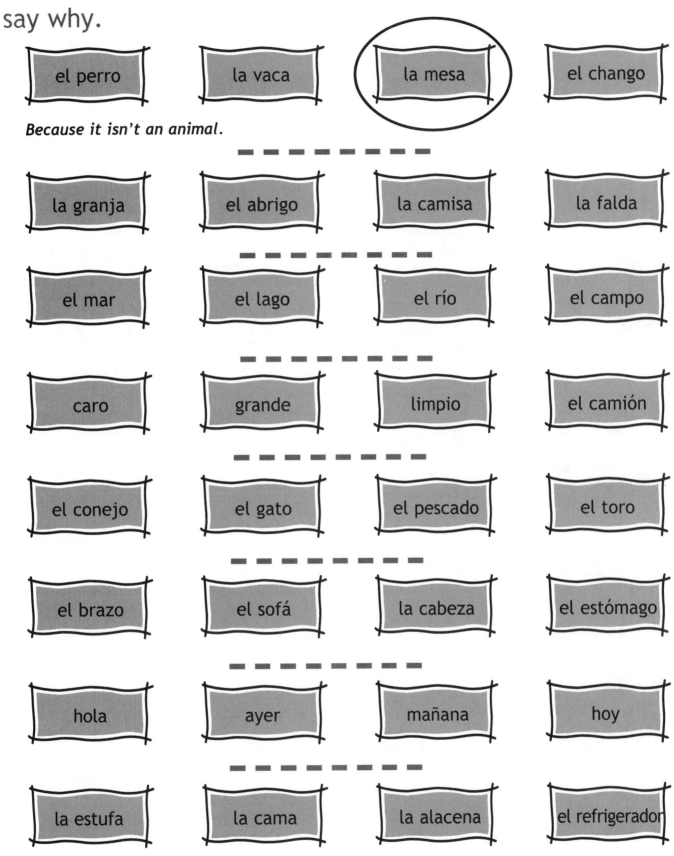

| el perro | la vaca | *(la mesa)* | el chango |

*Because it isn't an animal.*

- - - - - - - - -

| la granja | el abrigo | la camisa | la falda |

- - - - - - - -

| el mar | el lago | el río | el campo |

- - - - - - - -

| caro | grande | limpio | el camión |

- - - - - - -

| el conejo | el gato | el pescado | el toro |

- - - - - - - -

| el brazo | el sofá | la cabeza | el estómago |

- - - - - - - -

| hola | ayer | mañana | hoy |

- - - - - - -

| la estufa | la cama | la alacena | el refrigerador |

◎ **L**ook at the objects below for 30 seconds.

◎ **C**over the picture and try to remember all the objects.
Circle the Spanish words for those objects you remember.

la flor          el zapato          gracias          la puerta

el coche          no          aquí          el abrigo          el camión

el cinturón          la montaña          la silla          el caballo

el sombrero     el calcetín

la corbata          el ojo          la cama

la bufanda          el banco          el tapete          el chango

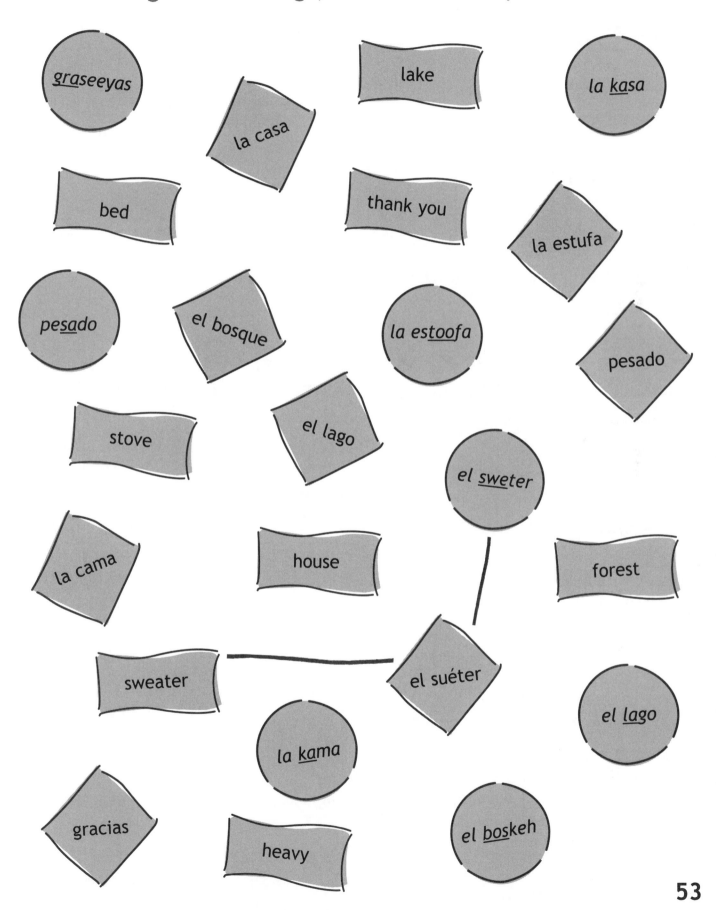

graseeyas

lake

la kasa

la casa

bed

thank you

la estufa

pesado

el bosque

la estoofa

pesado

stove

el lago

el sweter

la cama

house

forest

sweater

el suéter

el lago

la kama

gracias

heavy

el boskeh

# Fill in the English phrase at the bottom of the page.

| | | |
|---|---|---|
| el sofá (w) | el banco (g) | la oreja (t) |
| el abrigo (o) | el lago (a) | el puente (e) |
| ¿dónde? (m) | ¿cuánto? (l) | mañana (i) |
| la vaca (b) | la ventana (l) | la carnicería (h) |
| la casa (e) | la boca (a) | el perro (d) |
| el ojo (o) | la oreja (p) | el ratón (v) |
| la colina (n) | la granja (y) | el abrigo (r) |
| el conejo (n) | la calle (e) | la silla (s) |

English phrase: (w) ( ) ( ) ( )  ( ) ( ) ( ) ( ) !

Look at the two pictures and check (✔) the objects that are different in Picture B.

Picture A

Picture B

| la falda | ☐ |
| los pantalones | ☐ |
| la puerta | ☐ |
| el gato | ☐ |
| la silla | ☐ |
| el pescado | ☐ |
| el calcetín | ☐ |
| el perro | ☐ |

Now join the Spanish words to their English equivalents.

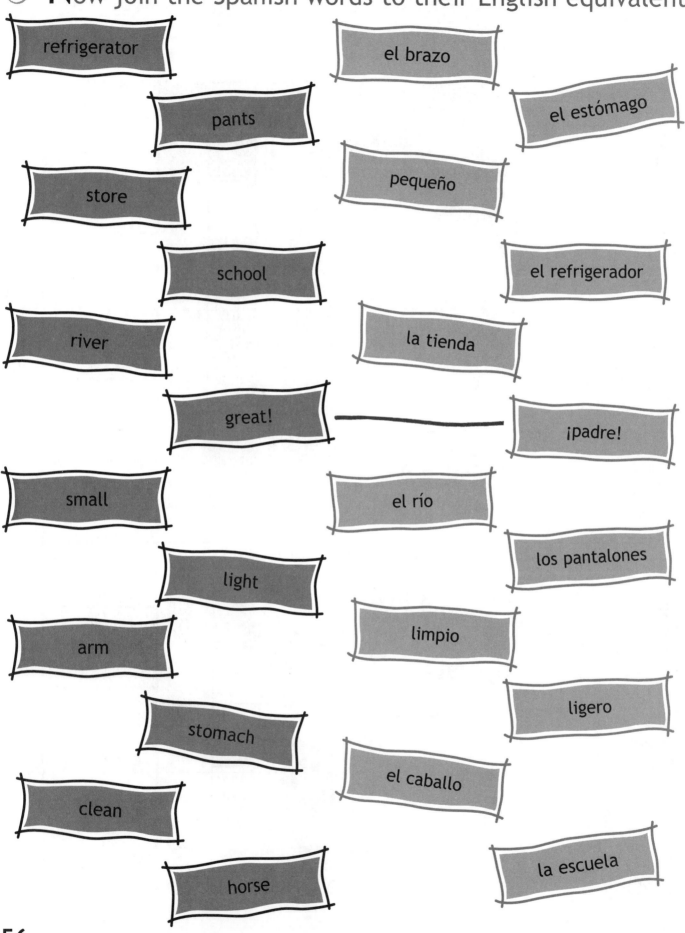

refrigerator

el brazo

pants

el estómago

store

pequeño

school

el refrigerador

river

la tienda

great! ————— ¡padre!

small

el río

light

los pantalones

arm

limpio

stomach

ligero

clean

el caballo

horse

la escuela

# Complete the crossword using the picture clues.

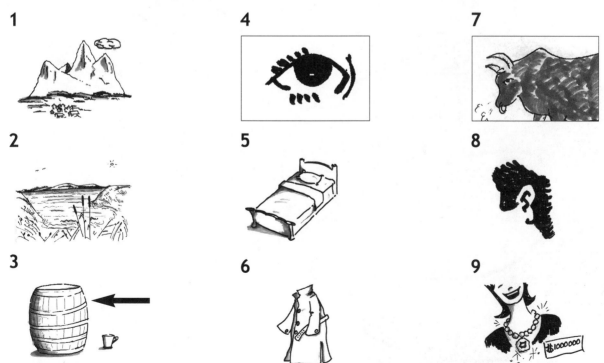

**1**

**2**

**3**

**4**

**5**

**6**

**7**

**8**

**9**

# Snake game.

- You will need a die and counter(s). You can challenge yourself to reach the finish or play with someone else. You have to throw the exact number to finish.

- Throw the die and move forward that number of spaces. When you land on a word you must pronounce it (with **el** or **la** if appropriate) and say what it means in English. If you can't, you have to go back to the square you came from.

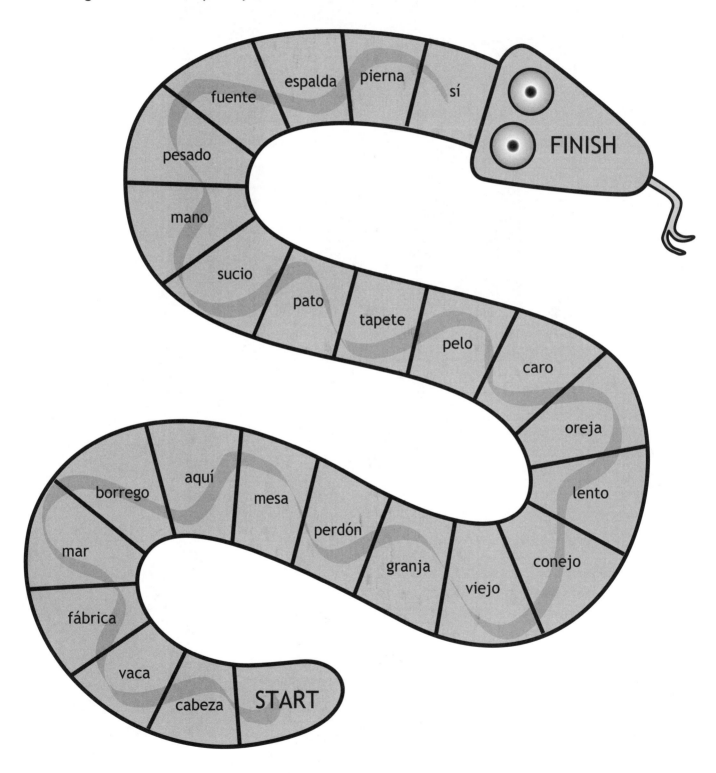

# ◎ **A**nswers

## ❶ **A**ROUND THE HOME

**Page 10 (top)**

See page 9 for correct picture.

**Page 10 (bottom)**

| | |
|---|---|
| door | la puerta |
| cupboard | la alacena |
| stove | la estufa |
| bed | la cama |
| table | la mesa |
| chair | la silla |
| refrigerator | el refrigerador |
| computer | la computadora |

**Page 11 (top)**

| | |
|---|---|
| silla | sofá |
| refrigerador | alacena |
| ventana | mesa |
| estufa | tapete |
| puerta | estante |

**Page 11 (bottom)**

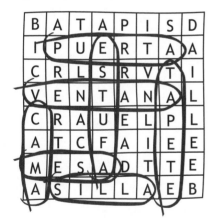

**Page 12**

**Page 13**

English word: window

## ❷ **C**LOTHES

**Page 15 (top)**

| | |
|---|---|
| el vestido | el suéter |
| el sombrero | el cinturón |
| la camisa | la corbata |
| la bufanda | la falda |

**Page 15 (bottom)**

**Page 16**

| | | |
|---|---|---|
| hat | el sombrero | *el sombrero* |
| shoe | el zapato | *el sapato* |
| sock | el calcetín | *el kalseteen* |
| scarf | la bufanda | *la boofanda* |
| tie | la corbata | *la korbata* |
| belt | el cinturón | *el seentooron* |
| coat | el abrigo | *el abreego* |
| pants | los pantalones | *los pantalones* |

**Page 17**

| | |
|---|---|
| sombrero (hat) | 1 |
| abrigo (coat) | 0 |
| cinturón (belt) | 2 |
| zapato (shoe) | 2 (1 pair) |
| pantalones (pants) | 1 |
| bufanda (scarf) | 1 |
| vestido (dress) | 0 |
| calcetín (sock) | 6 (3 pairs) |
| falda (skirt) | 0 |
| corbata (tie) | 2 |
| camisa (shirt) | 4 |
| suéter (sweater) | 1 |

**Page 18**

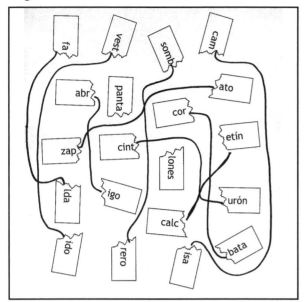

## ③ AROUND TOWN

**Page 20 (top)**

| | |
|---|---|
| truck | el camión |
| store | la tienda |
| factory | la fábrica |
| bench | el banco |
| car | el coche |
| fountain | la fuente |
| school | la escuela |
| house | la casa |

**Page 20 (bottom)**

| | |
|---|---|
| bicycle | 4 |
| bench | 7 |
| house | 2 |
| fountain | 6 |
| truck | 1 |
| road | 3 |
| car | 5 |

**Page 21**

1 el banco

2 el coche

3 la fuente

4 la fábrica

5 el camión

6 la escuela

7 la calle

8 la carnicería

9 la panadería

**Page 22**

English word: school

**Page 23**

| el | la |
|---|---|
| el banco | la bicicleta |
| el camión | la tienda |
| el coche | la panadería |
| | la casa |
| | la fuente |
| | la calle |
| | la carnicería |
| | la fábrica |
| | la escuela |

## ④ COUNTRYSIDE

**Page 25**

See page 24 for correct picture.

**Page 26**

| | | | |
|---|---|---|---|
| puente | ✔ | campo | ✔ |
| árbol | ✔ | bosque | ✔ |
| lluvia | ✘ | lago | ✘ |
| colina | ✘ | río | ✔ |
| montaña | ✔ | flor | ✔ |
| mar | ✘ | granja | ✘ |

**Page 27 (top)**

| | |
|---|---|
| la lluvia | la flor |
| el bosque | el río |
| el árbol | el lago |
| el mar | la colina |

**Page 27 (bottom)**

| | | |
|---|---|---|
| sea | el mar | *el mar* |
| lake | el lago | *el lago* |
| rain | la lluvia | *la l-yooveeya* |
| farm | la granja | *la granha* |
| flower | la flor | *la flor* |
| mountain | la montaña | *la montanya* |
| river | el río | *el reeyo* |
| field | el campo | *el kampo* |

# ❺ OPPOSITES

**Page 30**

| | |
|---|---|
| expensive | caro |
| big | grande |
| light | ligero |
| slow | lento |
| clean | limpio |
| inexpensive | barato |
| dirty | sucio |
| small | pequeño |
| heavy | pesado |
| new | nuevo |
| fast | rápido |
| old | viejo |

**Page 31**

English word: change

**Page 32**

Odd one outs are those which are not opposites:
pesado
pequeño
nuevo
sucio
lento
barato

**Page 33**

| | |
|---|---|
| old | nuevo |
| big | pequeño |
| new | viejo |
| slow | rápido |
| dirty | limpio |

| | |
|---|---|
| small | grande |
| heavy | ligero |
| clean | sucio |
| light | pesado |
| expensive | barato |
| inexpensive | caro |
| fast | lento |

# ❻ ANIMALS

**Page 35**

la vaca   el conejo   el pescado

el borrego   el perro   el chango

el caballo   el ratón   el gato

**Page 36**

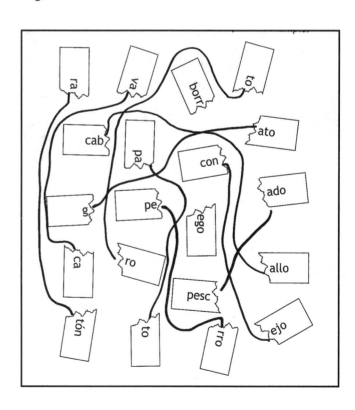

**Page 37**

| | | | |
|---|---|---|---|
| donkey | ✔ | mouse | ✘ |
| monkey | ✘ | cat | ✔ |
| sheep | ✔ | dog | ✘ |
| bull | ✔ | cow | ✔ |
| fish | ✔ | horse | ✘ |
| duck | ✘ | rabbit | ✔ |

**Page 38**

| | |
|---|---|
| monkey | el chango |
| cow | la vaca |
| mouse | el ratón |
| dog | el perro |
| sheep | el borrego |
| fish | el pescado |
| bull | el toro |
| donkey | el burro |
| cat | el gato |
| duck | el pato |
| rabbit | el conejo |
| horse | el caballo |

# ❼ PARTS OF THE BODY

**Page 40 (top)**

See page 39 for correct picture.

**Page 40 (bottom)**

| S | N | H | E | V | B | U | G |
|---|---|---|---|---|---|---|---|
| I | A | M | A | N | O | B | I |
| C | R | L | D | S | C | O | V |
| P | I | E | R | N | A | U | A |
| E | Z | A | U | I | L | C | N |
| L | N | N | A | R | I | S | E |
| O | R | E | J | A | L | E | E |
| L | E | Z | P | R | T | A | T |

You should have also drawn pictures of:
leg; mouth; ear; nose; hand; hair

**Page 41**

| el | la |
|---|---|
| el brazo | la nariz |
| el dedo | la cabeza |
| el estómago | la mano |
| el ojo | la pierna |
| el pelo | la boca |
| | la oreja |
| | la espalda |

**Page 42**

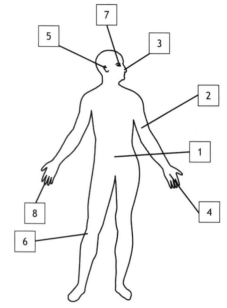

| | | | |
|---|---|---|---|
| 1 | el estómago | 2 | el brazo |
| 3 | la nariz | 4 | la mano |
| 5 | la oreja | 6 | la pierna |
| 7 | el ojo | 8 | el dedo |

**Page 43**

| | | |
|---|---|---|
| ear | la oreja | la oreha |
| hair | el pelo | el pelo |
| hand | la mano | la mano |
| stomach | el estómago | el estomago |
| arm | el brazo | el braso |
| back | la espalda | la espalda |
| finger | el dedo | el dedo |
| leg | la pierna | la pee-yerna |

## ⑧ USEFUL EXPRESSIONS

**Page 45 (top)**

| | |
|---|---|
| great! | ¡padre! |
| yes | sí |
| yesterday | ayer |
| where? | ¿dónde? |
| today | hoy |
| here | aquí |
| please | por favor |
| no | no |

**Page 45 (bottom)**

| | |
|---|---|
| ¿cuánto? | hoy |
| gracias | adiós |
| perdón | ¡padre! |
| hola | ahí |
| mañana | ahora |

**Page 46**

English word: please

**Page 47**

**Page 48**

| | | |
|---|---|---|
| yes | sí | *see* |
| hello | hola | *ola* |
| here | aquí | *akee* |
| sorry | perdón | *perdon* |
| please | por favor | *por favor* |
| there | ahí | *ayee* |
| thank you | gracias | *graseeyas* |
| tomorrow | mañana | *manyana* |

## ● ROUND-UP

**Page 49**

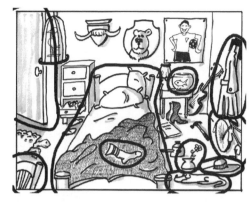

**Page 50**

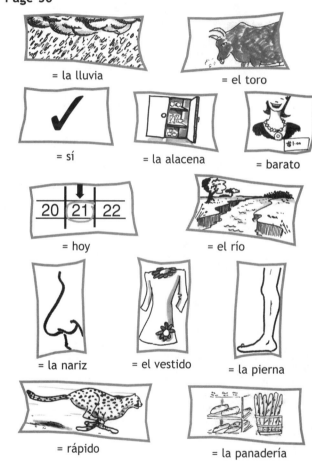

= la lluvia

= el toro

= sí

= la alacena

= barato

= hoy

= el río

= la nariz

= el vestido

= la pierna

= rápido

= la panadería

**Page 51**

la mesa (Because it isn't an animal.)

la granja (Because it isn't an item of clothing.)

el campo (Because it isn't connected with water.)

el camión (Because it isn't a descriptive word.)

el pescado (Because it lives in water/doesn't have legs.)

el sofá (Because it isn't a part of the body.)

hola (Because it isn't an expression of time.)

la cama (Because you wouldn't find it in the kitchen.)

## Page 52

Words that appear in the picture:

la corbata
el coche
la flor
el zapato
el sombrero
el camión
el chango
el tapete
la silla
el cinturón
la bufanda

## Page 53

| sweater | el suéter | el _sweter_ |
| lake | el lago | el _lago_ |
| thank you | gracias | _graseeyas_ |
| bed | la cama | la _kama_ |
| house | la casa | la _kasa_ |
| forest | el bosque | el _boskeh_ |
| stove | la estufa | la es_toofa_ |
| heavy | pesado | pes_ado_ |

## Page 54

English phrase: well done!

## Page 55

| la falda | ✗ |
| los pantalones | ✔ (shade) |
| la puerta | ✔ (handle) |
| el gato | ✗ |
| la silla | ✔ (back) |
| el pescado | ✔ (direction) |
| el calcetín | ✔ (pattern) |
| el perro | ✗ |

## Page 56

| refrigerator | el refrigerador |
| pants | los pantalones |
| store | la tienda |
| school | la escuela |
| river | el río |
| great! | ¡padre! |
| small | pequeño |
| light | ligero |
| arm | el brazo |
| stomach | el estómago |
| clean | limpio |
| horse | el caballo |

## Page 57

## Page 58

Here are the English equivalents of the word, in order from START to FINISH:

| head | la cabeza | ear | la oreja |
|------|-----------|-----|----------|
| cow | la vaca | expensive | caro |
| factory | la fábrica | hair | el pelo |
| sea | el mar | rug | el tapete |
| sheep | el borrego | duck | el pato |
| here | aquí | dirty | sucio |
| table | la mesa | hand | la mano |
| sorry | perdón | heavy | pesado |
| farm | la granja | fountain | la fuente |
| old | viejo | back | la espalda |
| rabbit | el conejo | leg | la pierna |
| slow | lento | yes | sí |

| la computadora | la ventana |
| la mesa | la alacena |
| el refrigerador | la silla |
| el sofá | la estufa |
| la puerta | la cama |
| el estante | el tapete |

| window | computer |
|--------|----------|
| cupboard | table |
| chair | refrigerator |
| stove | sofa |
| bed | door |
| rug | shelf |

el cinturón

el abrigo

la falda

el sombrero

la corbata

el zapato

el suéter

la camisa

la bufanda

el calcetín

los pantalones

el vestido

| coat | belt |
|------|------|
| hat | skirt |
| shoe | tie |
| shirt | sweater |
| sock | scarf |
| dress | pants |

| | |
|---|---|
| la escuela | el coche |
| la calle | el camión |
| la fábrica | la tienda |
| el banco | la bicicleta |
| la carnicería | la panadería |
| la fuente | la casa |

| car | school |
|-----|--------|
| truck | road |
| store | factory |
| bicycle | bench |
| baker | butcher |
| house | fountain |

el lago

el bosque

la colina

el mar

la montaña

el árbol

la lluvia

la flor

el puente

el río

la granja

el campo

| forest | lake |
| --- | --- |
| sea | hill |
| tree | mountain |
| flower | rain |
| river | bridge |
| field | farm |

| | |
|---|---|
| pesado | ligero |
| grande | pequeño |
| viejo | nuevo |
| rápido | lento |
| limpio | sucio |
| barato | caro |

light

heavy

small

big

new

old

slow

fast

dirty

clean

expensive

inexpensive

el pato

el gato

el ratón

la vaca

el conejo

el perro

el caballo

el chango

el toro

el pescado

el burro

el borrego

| | |
|---|---|
| cat | duck |
| cow | mouse |
| dog | rabbit |
| monkey | horse |
| fish | bull |
| sheep | donkey |

| | |
|---|---|
| el brazo | el dedo |
| la cabeza | la boca |
| la oreja | la pierna |
| la mano | el estómago |
| el ojo | el pelo |
| la nariz | la espalda |

| finger | arm |
|--------|-----|
| mouth | head |
| leg | ear |
| stomach | hand |
| hair | eye |
| back | nose |

| | |
|---|---|
| por favor | gracias |
| sí | no |
| hola | adiós |
| ayer | hoy |
| mañana | ¿dónde? |
| aquí | ahí |
| perdón | ¿cuánto? |
| ¡padre! | ahora |

| thank you | please |
|---|---|
| no | yes |
| goodbye | hello |
| today | yesterday |
| where? | tomorrow |
| there | here |
| how much? | sorry! |
| now | great! |